The Milky Way is the galaxy that contains our Solar System

IF YOU WANT TO SEE IT JUST LOOK UP

The Milky Way contains hundreds of billions of stars

like our sun

And like our sun, most of these stars have at least one planet orbiting them

Our planet Earth is located between the center of the Milky Way and its edge.

Our solar system consists of eight planets which all orbit around our home star: the Sun.

These eight planets are:

 Mercury

 Venus

 Earth

 Mars

 Jupiter

 Saturn

 Uranus

 Neptune

01 MERCURY

Mercury i the smallest in our solar system, and it's the closest to the sun. Mercury's size is only a little bit larger than the Earth's moon.

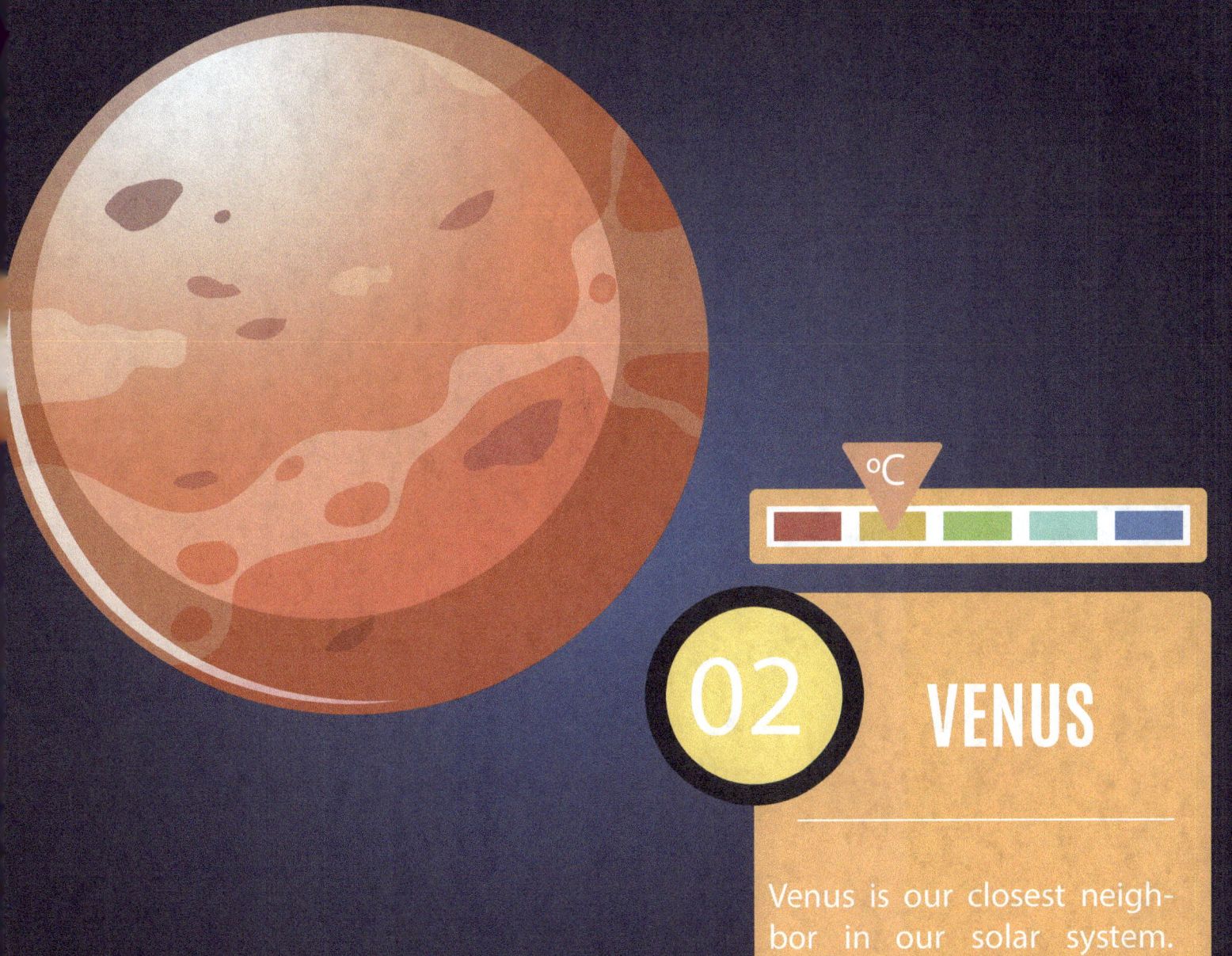

02 VENUS

Venus is our closest neighbor in our solar system. Although very similar in size and structure to our Earth, Venus spins more slowly and in the opposite direction than most of the planets in our solar system.

03 EARTH

Earth is the only known planet to support life and was formed around 4.54 billion years ago.

°C

04 MARS

There have been 40 missions to Mars, but only 18 of the missions were successful.
The dust storms on Mars are so large that they are considered to be the biggest in the solar system.

°C

05 JUPITER

If Jupiter had been 80 times more massive it would have become our second sun in the solar system.

Jupiter holds the title of being the solar system's fourth brightest object.

06 SATURN

There are only five planets that can be seen from Earth with the naked eye, Saturn is one of them.
Most planets are somewhat spherical in shape, but Saturn is flatter; in fact it's the flattest of any planet in the solar system.

07 URANUS

Uranus has the coldest temperatures of all of the planets, hitting as low as -224 degrees C.

°C

08 NEPTUNE

Neptune has a Great Dark Spot that is the size of our Earth and a Small Dark Spot that is almost the size of our moon.

°C

Help Astronaut Liam get to his spaceship

Now let us see some interesting facts about our solar system

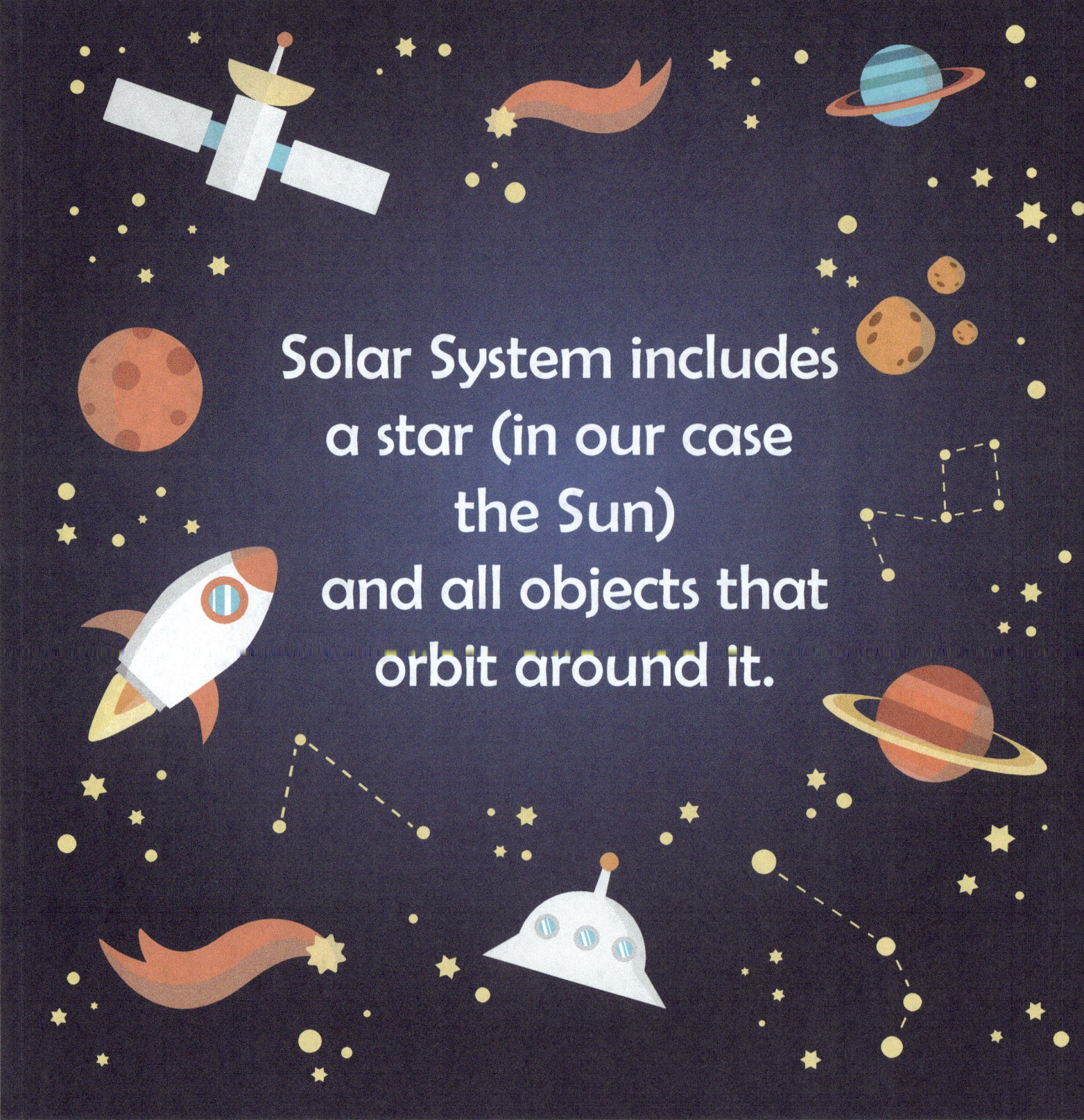

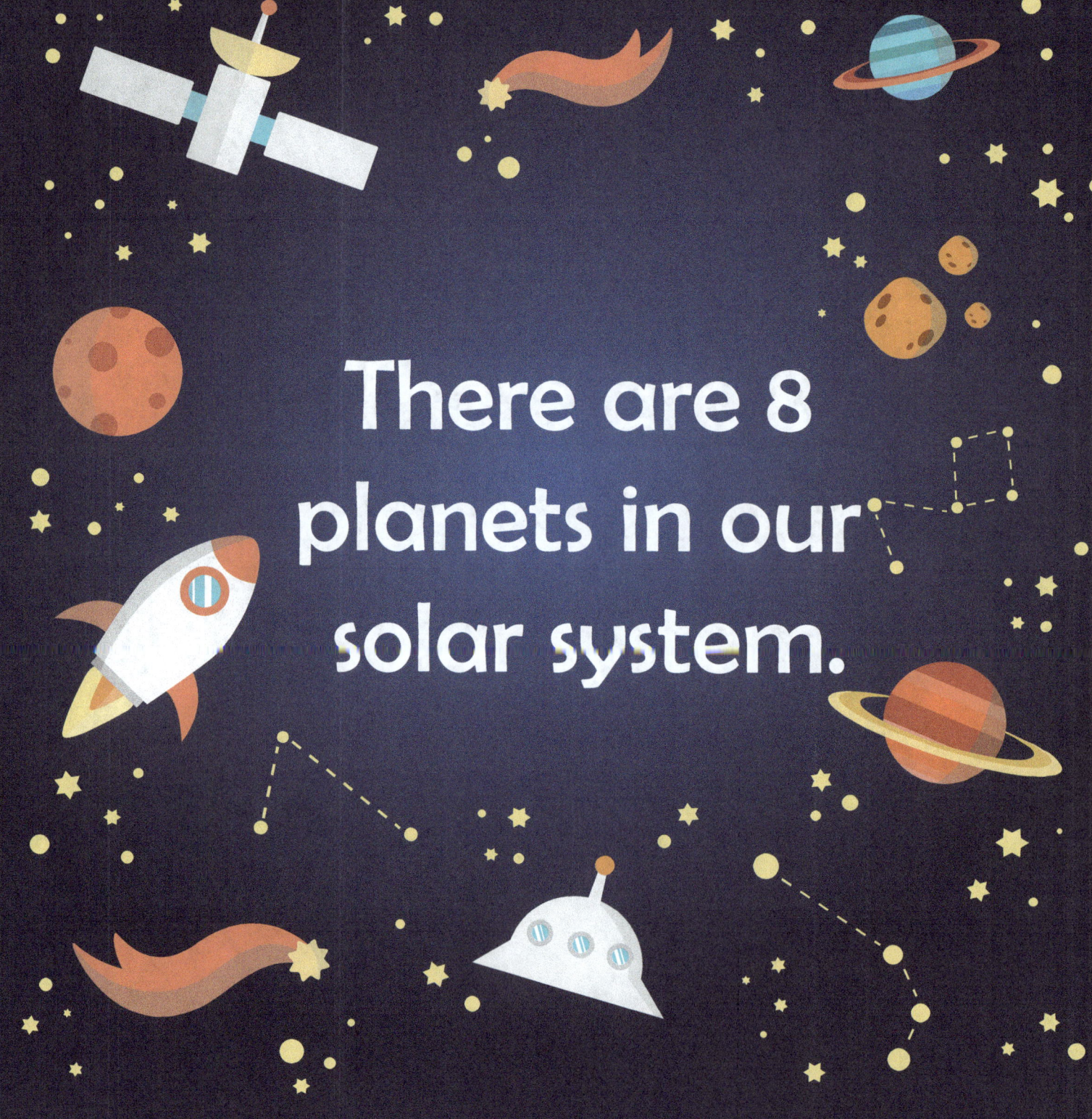

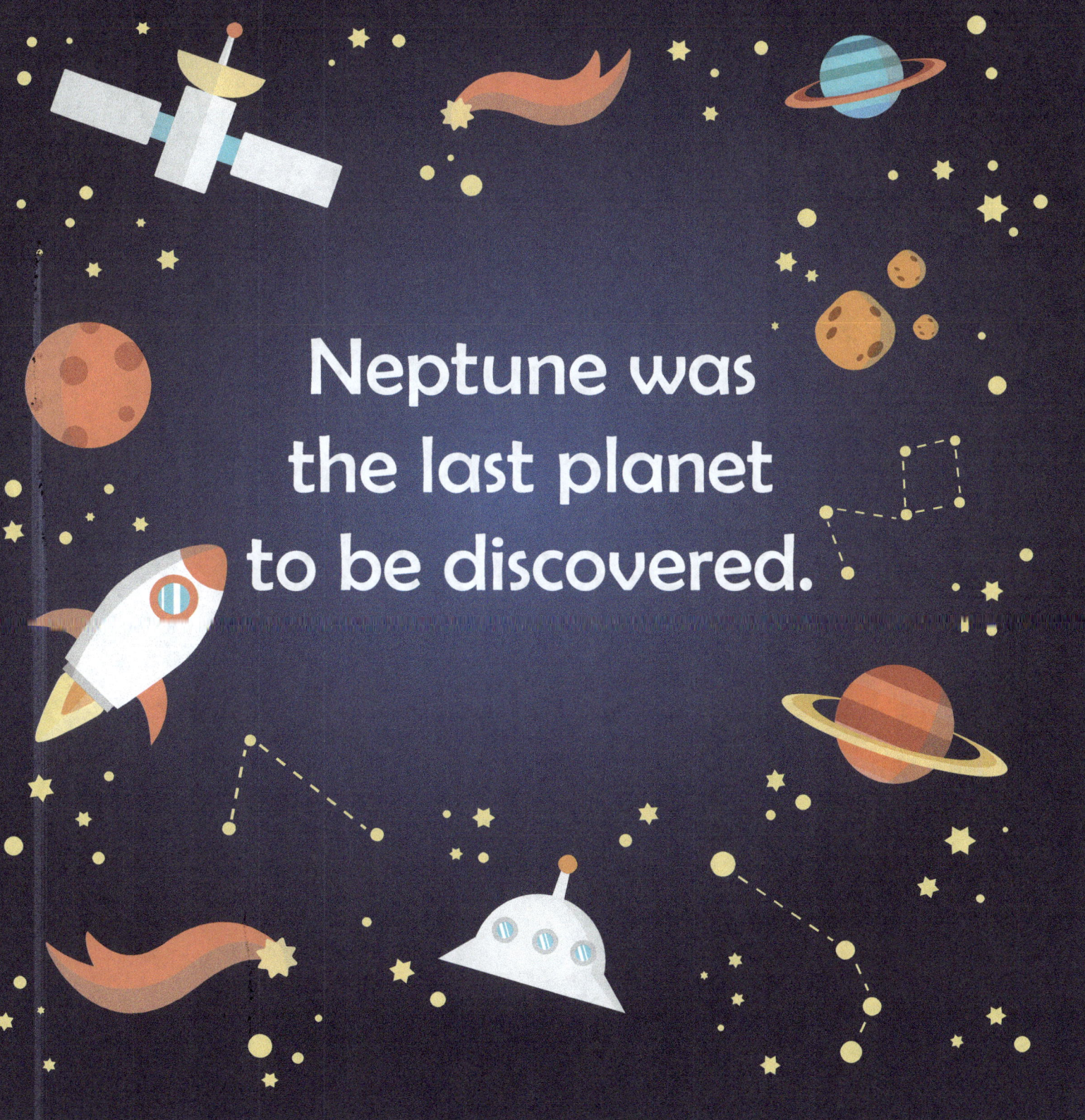

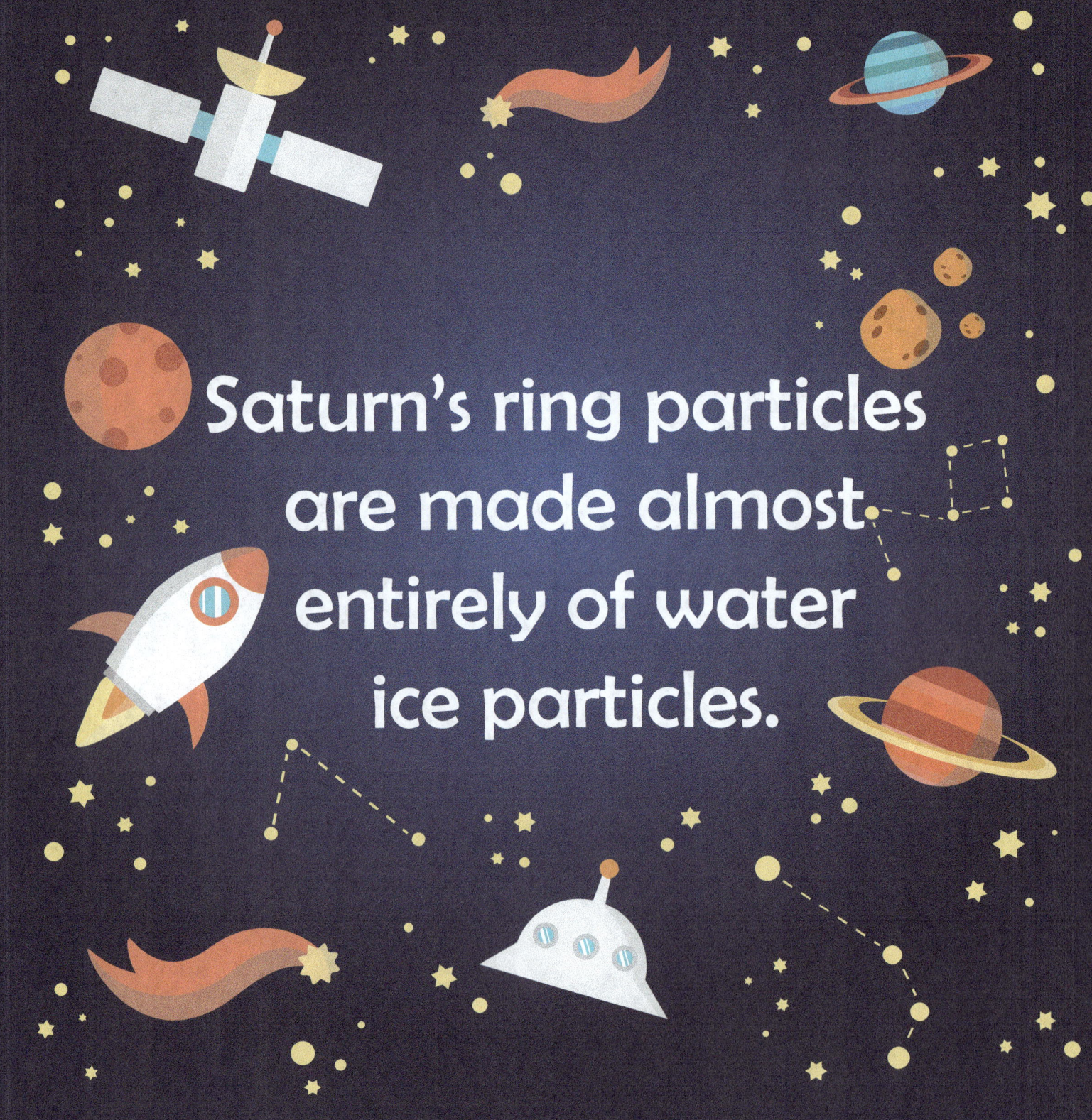

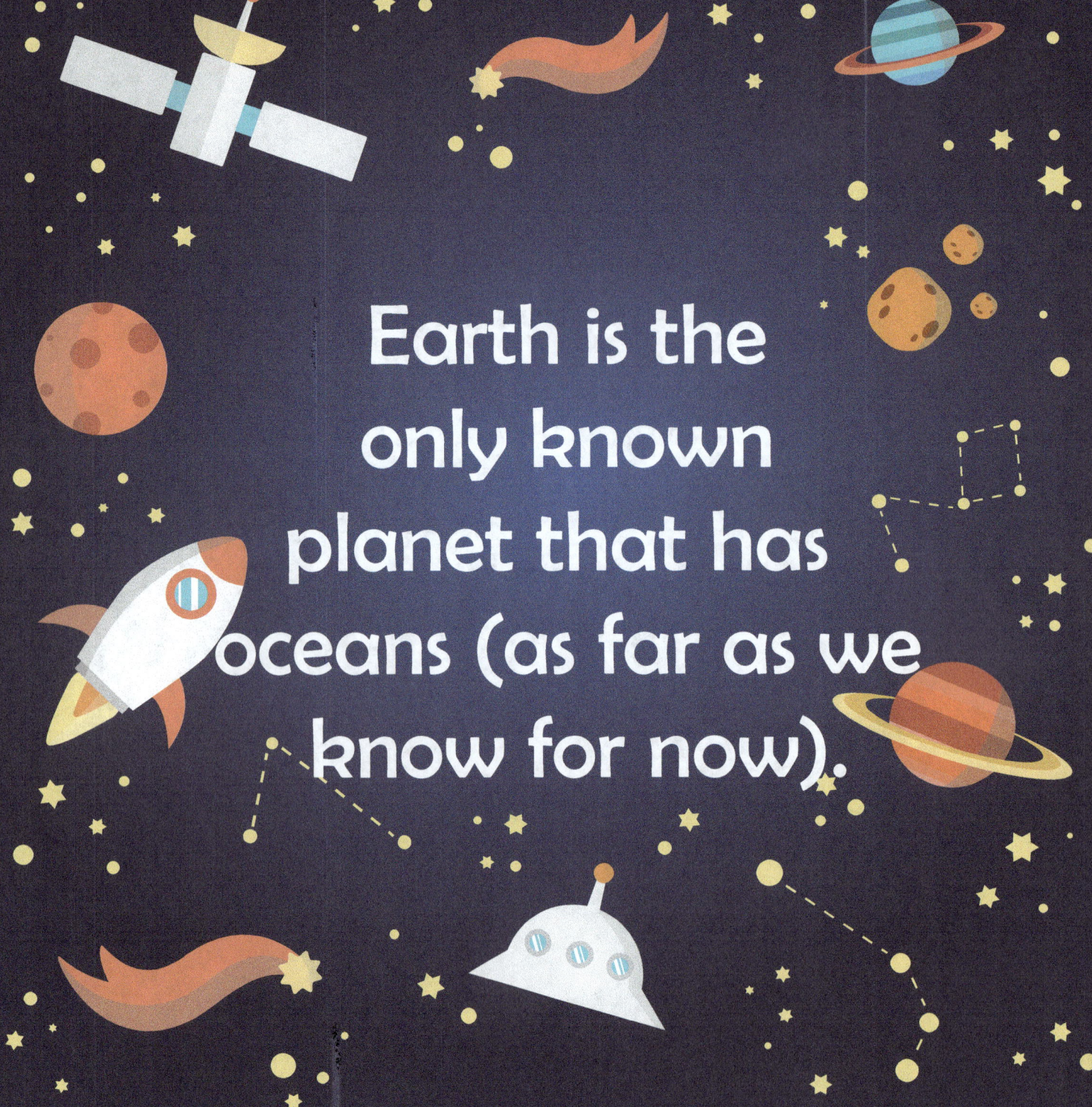

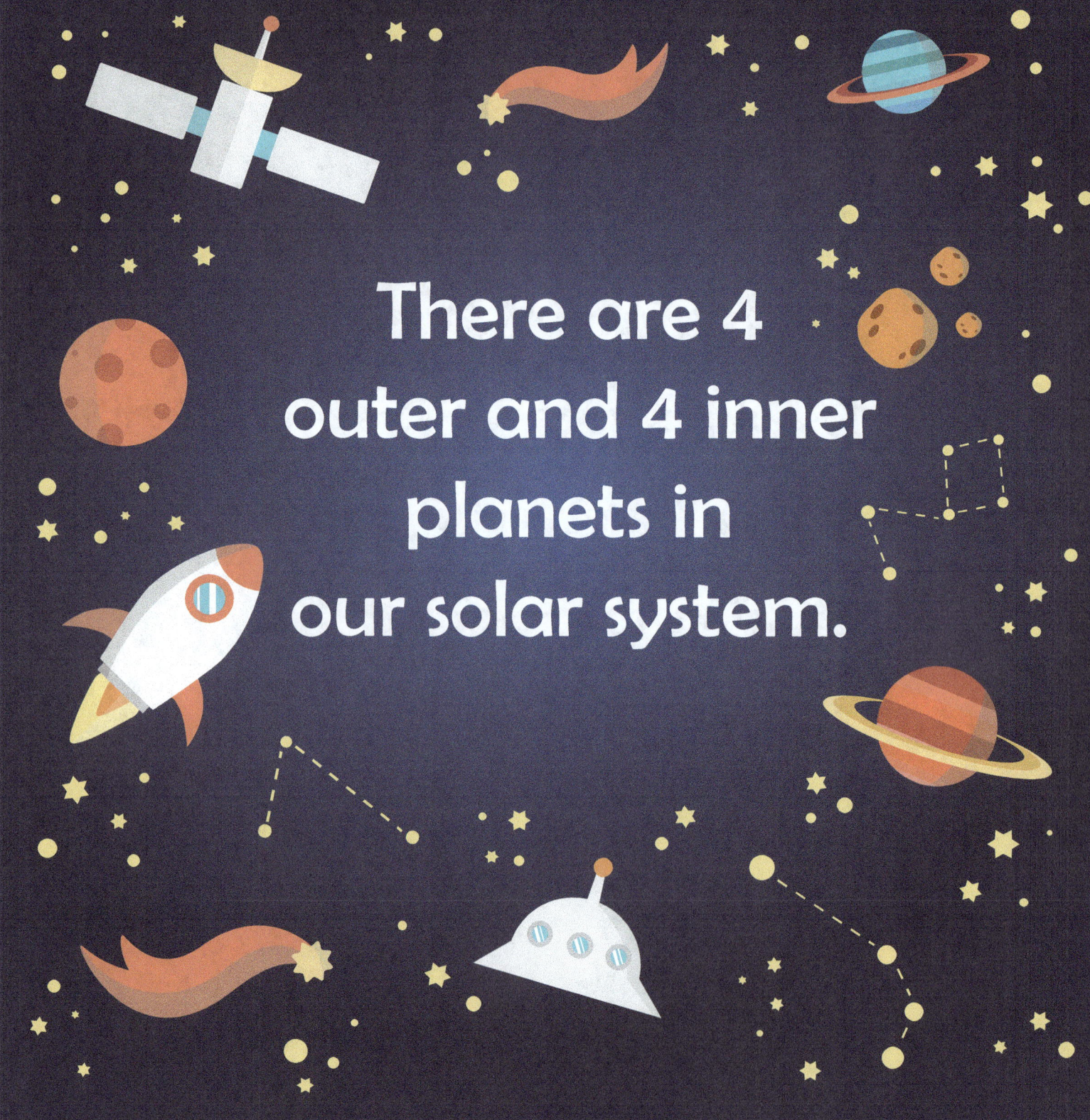

www.ingramcontent.com/pod-product-compliance
Lightning Source LLC
Chambersburg PA
CBHW081629100526
44590CB00021B/3662